# NORTH AMERICAN NATURAL RESOURCES

# COAL

W9-ATY-560

# North American Natural Resources

Coal

Copper

Freshwater Resources

Gold and Silver

Iron

Marine Resources

Natural Gas

Oil

Renewable Energy

Salt

Timber and Forest Products

Uranium

# NORTH AMERICAN NATURAL RESOURCES

# COAL

## Steve Parker

MASON CREST

Mason Crest
450 Parkway Drive, Suite D
Broomall, PA 19008
www.masoncrest.com

MTM Publishing, Inc.
435 West 23rd Street, #8C
New York, NY 10011
www.mtmpublishing.com

President: Valerie Tomaselli
Vice President, Book Development: Hilary Poole
Designer: Annemarie Redmond
Illustrator: Richard Garratt
Copyeditor: Peter Jaskowiak
Editorial Assistant: Andrea St. Aubin

Series ISBN: 978-1-4222-3378-8
ISBN: 978-1-4222-3379-5
Ebook ISBN: 978-1-4222-8553-4

Library of Congress Cataloging-in-Publication Data
Parker, Steve, 1952-
  [Coal (2015)]
  Coal / by Steve Parker.
      pages cm. — (North American natural resources)
  Includes index.
   ISBN 978-1-4222-3379-5 (hardback) — ISBN 978-1-4222-3378-8 (series) —
ISBN 978-1-4222-8553-4 (ebook)
 1.  Coal—North America—Juvenile literature.  I. Title.
  TN801.P3723 2015
  333.8'220973—dc23
                              2015005854

Printed and bound in the United States of America.

First printing
9 8 7 6 5 4 3 2 1

# TABLE OF CONTENTS

## Key Icons to Look for:

 **Words to Understand:** These words with their easy-to-understand definitions will increase the reader's understanding of the text, while building vocabulary skills.

 **Sidebars:** This boxed material within the main text allows readers to build knowledge, gain insights, explore possibilities, and broaden their perspectives by weaving together additional information to provide realistic and holistic perspectives.

 **Research Projects:** Readers are pointed toward areas of further inquiry connected to each chapter. Suggestions are provided for projects that encourage deeper research and analysis.

 **Text-Dependent Questions:** These questions send the reader back to the text for more careful attention to the evidence presented there.

 **Series Glossary of Key Terms:** This back-of-the-book glossary contains terminology used throughout the series. Words found here increase the reader's ability to read and comprehend higher-level books and articles in this field.

*Note to Educator:* *As publishers, we feel it's our role to give young adults the tools they need to thrive in a global society. To encourage a more worldly perspective, this book contains both imperial and metric measurements as well as references to a wider global context. We hope to expose the readers to the most common conversions they will come across outside of North America.*

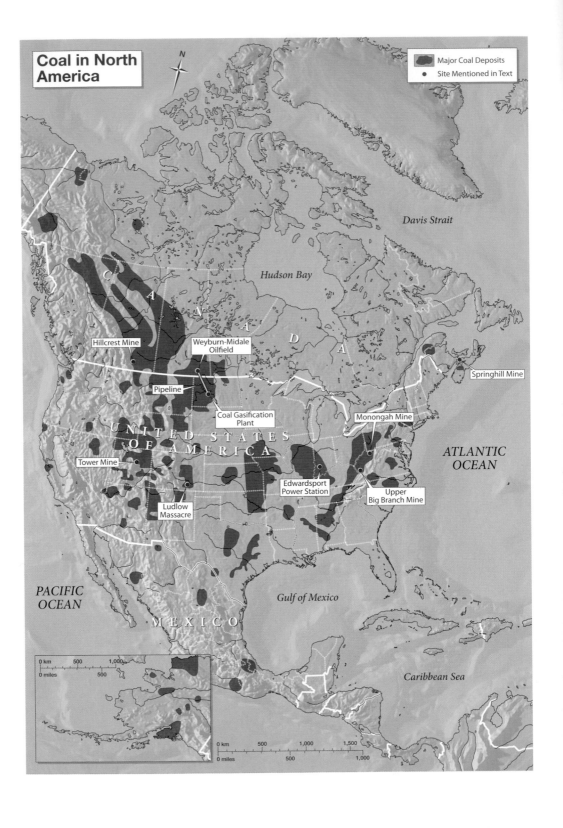

# Coal in North America

Major Coal Deposits

Site Mentioned in Text

*Davis Strait*

*Hudson Bay*

C A N A D A

Hillcrest Mine

Weyburn-Midale Oilfield

Springhill Mine

Pipeline

Coal Gasification Plant

Monongah Mine

U N I T E D   S T A T E S
O F   A M E R I C A

ATLANTIC OCEAN

Tower Mine

Edwardsport Power Station

Upper Big Branch Mine

Ludlow Massacre

PACIFIC OCEAN

M E X I C O

*Gulf of Mexico*

*Caribbean Sea*

0 km   500   1,000
0 miles       500

0 km   500   1,000   1,500
0 miles       500       1,000

# INTRODUCTION

**N**orth America has the largest coal reserves in the world. Most estimates show that they will last for more than 200 years. But coal's role as a popular fuel in North America is changing.

One reason is that, when burned, coal is relatively "dirty." It produces more emissions, as gases and particles, than do natural gas or petroleum fuels. The emissions include carbon dioxide, a major greenhouse gas that contributes to the process of global warming. This is affecting the

**A corridor in a large coal mine. (Aniuszka/Dreamstime)**

whole Earth—its atmosphere, oceans, soils, plants, animals, and people. In the United States, coal provides about one-fifth of all energy use, mostly as electricity, but burning it produces one-third of all carbon dioxide emissions. Burning coal also releases other polluting substances as well as harmful *heavy metals* such as arsenic and mercury. All of these substances have caused widespread environmental problems in the past.

The coal industry is trying to change with the times, however. The latest coal-fired power plants are many times more efficient at turning coal energy into electrical energy. They also use advanced technologies, such as filters and carbon capture, to reduce pollution. And there are new ways of using coal, such as converting it into gas and liquid fuels and many other products. Supporters of coal say that it can be used in new, more flexible and less polluting ways. They argue that it can provide North America with a valuable, reliable, and plentiful natural resource for centuries to come.

## Chapter One

# HOW COAL FORMED

oal, like natural gas and petroleum oil, is a resource known as a *fossil fuel*. It formed millions of years ago from the remains of living things, altered and preserved deep in the ground. This happened especially during the Carboniferous period, from 359 to 299 million years ago. The time span is named after its **carbon**-rich remains (carbon is the main substance in coal).

### Words to Understand

**anaerobic:** occurring without oxygen.

**bituminous:** containing the thick, sticky, dark, tarry substance called bitumen or asphalt.

**carbon:** a pure chemical substance or element found in great amounts in living and once-living things.

**macerals:** microscopic particles or units in coal, made from the changed, fossilized remains of plants.

**reserves:** amounts in store, to be used in the future.

**stagnant:** inactive or stale.

The ancient ancestors of this horsetail fern, called cordaitales, eventually became coal.

# The Age of Coal

During the early Carboniferous period, about 359–323 million years ago, the Earth looked very different than it does today. It was warmer, and the air was more humid, with more oxygen gas in the atmosphere. Sea and freshwater levels were higher, too, with vast swampy areas.

Carboniferous plants included massive, woody-stemmed trees, some over 100 feet (30 meters) tall. Some of those huge Carboniferous plants were scale trees, which have very small cousins surviving today, the club mosses; both belong to the lycopsid group. Others were seed ferns or pteridosperms, a varied group similar to modern ferns. There were also giant Carboniferous versions of today's horsetails, and tall conifer-like trees known as cordaitales, now extinct. All these, and many more, lived and died in the steamy, swampy forests—and became coal.

In the late Carboniferous period (323–299 million years ago) the world's climates became cooler and drier, and sea levels fell. But great forests of ancient tree-sized plants continued to thrive and form enormous quantities of vegetation that would become coal. This time span is sometimes called the Pennsylvanian period, for the US state where large amounts of the Carboniferous coal called anthracite are located.

## Carboniferous Animals

Like the plants of this period, Carboniferous animals were also giants. Dragonfly-like griffinflies had wings almost 30 inches (75 centimeters) across, millipedes were 6 feet (almost 2 meters) long, and fierce amphibians—cousins of today's salamanders—resembled crocodiles 10 feet (3 meters) in length. Dinosaurs, birds, and mammals were far in the future.

**A modern fire salamander.**

## Early Stages: Peat and Lignite

The transformation of vast prehistoric piles of soggy, semi-rotting plants into coal was not a simple one-stage process. It was slow and continuous, with greatly varied conditions of temperature, types of plants, amount of moisture, and more, including how deep the remains were buried. This makes coal different in every place it is now found. But overall, there were several stages in coal formation, or coalification: peat, lignite, sub-**bituminous** coal, bituminous coal, and anthracite. Types of coal matter because each type contains a different level of carbon.  The higher the carbon content, the more heat energy produced when the coal is burned.

**Piles of peat dug up in Ireland.**

First, the newly dead plants piled up into a squishy mass called peat. This happens today in peat bogs, mires, marshes, and swamps around the world. Depending on growing conditions, it took between 5,000 and 100,000 years to make a layer of peat one yard (0.91 meters) deep. Peat contains lots of water, along with many plant parts, such as roots, leaves, shoots, and bark, all in various stages of rotting or decay. But the water tends to be **stagnant** and low in oxygen. Without plentiful oxygen, the usual process of decay slows down. One of the products is the gas methane, familiar as the main substance in natural gas  and as deadly "firedamp" in coal mines, as discussed in chapter five.

As more great plants grew and died, the peat got buried by more peat, and by other layers, too, including mud or silt from floods. The peat was changed by being compressed, which also generated heat. Its water was driven off. It altered in the **anaerobic** conditions due to the action of microbes called bacteria. The soggy, squashy peat changed into a drier, harder, more crumbly substance called lignite, or brown coal. This is a "young" or "immature" form of coal.

## Middle Stages: Toward Bituminous Coal

Many millions of years passed. Greater compression from layers collecting on top, and higher temperatures from the deeper burial, caused more change. The lignite gradually transformed into a harder, darker material known as sub-bituminous coal, or black lignite.

With yet more time, more pressure, more heat, and more chemical changes, sub-bituminous coal continued to change into the next form, bituminous coal. This is what many people picture when asked to think of coal: hard, dark brown or black chunks. Formation of bituminous coal needs temperatures of about 250–500°F (120–260°C), which usually means burial to 10,000 feet (3,000 meters) or more. On average, it took a layer of peat 10 feet (3 meters) deep to make a layer of bituminous coal 1 foot (30 centimeters) deep. Sometimes lumps of coal split to reveal fossil shapes or impressions of fern fronds, scale tree bark, and similar plant parts from those distant times.

More than 90 percent of all coal mined in North America is bituminous and sub-bituminous. America's eastern and mid-Atlantic coalfields are mainly bituminous,

**Bituminous coal.**

while Alaska and Western states yield sub-bituminous coal. Canada has the world's 12th-largest **reserves** of coal. Most Canadian coal is mined in the west, in British Columbia and Alberta, with smaller amounts in Saskatchewan, New Brunswick, and Nova Scotia. Mining in Mexico, which has less than 0.2 percent of world reserves, is mainly in the northeastern province of Coahuila, south of Texas.

## Later Stages: Anthracite and Graphite

In those places where coal formation continues past the bituminous stage, the next form is anthracite. This is "old" or "mature" coal. It is very hard, heavy, dry, black, and shiny. It also has the most energy content, which is linked to its carbon content. It burns with little smoke and fewer forms of pollution than other kinds of coal. Most anthracite in the United States comes from an area called the Coal Region in northeastern Pennsylvania.

The different forms of coal are differentiated by their carbon content and heat (or energy) content, which is measured in the heat or energy units called BTUs (British Thermal Units) per pound in weight, as follows:

- Peat is 20–40 percent carbon, with a heat content of 2,000–6,000 BTUs per pound.
- Lignite is 25–35 percent carbon, with a heat content of 4,000–8,000 BTUs per pound.
- Sub-bituminous coal is 35–45 percent carbon, with a heat content of 8,000–12,000 BTUs per pound.
- Bituminous coal is 60–85 percent carbon, with a heat content of 10,000–15,000 BTUs per pound.
- Anthracite is 90–98 percent carbon, with a heat content of up to 15,000 BTUs per pound.

**The Morden Mine on Vancouver Island, British Colombia, was built in 1913. No longer active, the mine is now on Canada's list of historic places.**

For comparison, gasoline has a heat content of 20,400 BTUs, diesel is nearer 19,300 BTUs, and seasoned wood has a value of 5,000–8,000 BTUs.

Of course, these are all averages. Each source of coal is tested and graded for its mineral and microscopic structure, based on structures called **macerals**, its energy yield, and for various contents such as sulfur, water, and traces of substances such as mercury and arsenic.

## Coal Times and Places

Much North American coal was formed during the Carboniferous period, but almost every time span saw coal formation after the first small, moss-like plants invaded the land. Some sub-bituminous coal in the western United States date to the Triassic and Jurassic periods (252–201 and 201–145 million years ago, respectively). Some Canadian coal formed more recently during the Cretaceous period (145–66 million years ago). Large amounts of coal in Wyoming date to the Cretaceous and early Paleogene periods, making it 130–50 million years old.

No matter when or where coal formed, it is sometimes called "buried sunshine," because it contains carbon-based substances that got their energy from sunlight. When coal burns today, it is releasing that prehistoric light energy, partly in the form of light again, and also as heat.

## Macerals

A high-power microscope shows that most rocks are made of mineral crystals and grains. In coal, similar tiny particles from the original living plant matter are called macerals. There are several main kinds, and their numbers and proportions give the coal its features.
- **Vitrinite macerals** are broken-down remains of harder plant parts like trunks, stems, and roots.
- **Liptinite macerals** come from softer plant parts such as leaves, buds, saps, and resins.
- **Inertite** is the fossilization product of charcoal, or plants that had burned in natural wildfires that swept through the ancient forests.

## TEXT-DEPENDENT QUESTIONS

1.  What are the stages of coalification?
2.  Why is the Carboniferous period so named?
3.  What are macerals?

## RESEARCH PROJECTS

1.  Look up further information on life during the Carboniferous period and the kinds of fossils found in its coal. Are there any flowers or mammals?
2.  Find out more about the links between the US state of Pennsylvania and the time span called the Pennsylvanian period.

## Chapter Two

# MINING COAL

Coal is extracted, or taken out of the ground, by mining. The earliest coal miners were not only men, but also women and children, who hacked at the coal with simple tools like stone flint choppers, animal horns and antlers, and early iron axes. Today's North American mines are highly technical and utilize some of the biggest machines in the world. But the work is still a very tough and physical, with many possible dangers.

Coal tended to form in horizontal layers, called coal seams, deep below the surface. Over millions of years since, great earth movements have lifted up rocks and coal seams to build mountains, cracked them open with earthquakes, and tilted them at angles; they have also been worn down by sun, rain, and other forces. So coal is now found at all kinds of depths, from thousands of feet down to exposed at the Earth's surface. There are basically two ways of mining it, surface and underground.

## Finding Coal

There are several ways to locate an area with plentiful coal, called a coalfield. Most simply, it is seen at the surface as a hard, dark rock. Walking or driving across an area, or flying overhead, may be enough to locate surface coal seams. Satellite photographs can also show their dark bands and patches. These areas are known as exposed coalfields.

There are several ways to find coalfields hidden under the surface. One of the most effective and least costly is the **seismic** survey. Shock waves or seismic vibrations

**The black band in this photo is a coal seam in a bank of soil.**

are sent down into the ground where they are reflected or redirected by various rock layers, in different ways, back to the surface. The echoed or returning waves are picked up by devices called seismometers, which measure their strength, time delay, and other features. The seismic survey is one of several methods that reveal the physical features of what is underground.

There are other surface methods to locate coal. Devices called gravimeters measure tiny changes in Earth's gravitational pull that are caused by different kinds of rocks. Magnetometers sense similar changes in the Earth's natural magnetic field. Chemical sensors can pick up faint traces of methane seeping up through the rocks from deep coal.

## Test Boreholes

If signs look good, the exploration company may drill some **boreholes**. This is done in a similar way as that used to search for petroleum oil and natural gas (see other titles in this series). The boreholes are spaced out to find the depth and extent of the coalfield.  Now and then, devices may be lowered into the borehole. These include "sniffers" for gases such as methane, counters to detect any natural rays or radiation from the rock, and seismic vibration producers to send out shock waves.

A seismograph records vibrations from below ground.

As information mounts about the area, depth, and quality of the coal seams, the mining company decides if and when to begin mining. Mine planners make many decisions, including which kinds of surface or underground mining to carry out, what machinery needed, and where to put access roads and camps for the workers. They must also gauge the effects of the mine on the local surroundings and environment, get permission from landowners, determine the likelihood of people protesting, costs, time schedules, and how much coal might sell for when it arrives, among other aspects of the operation.

## Surface Mining

At a surface mine, any layer of soil and rocks, called the *overburden*, is removed to reveal the coal. Enormous machines like diggers, bulldozers, and excavators lift and move the overburden, which is usually stored to put back later when the area is repaired or "rehabilitated." Explosives may loosen very hard rock.

Then **excavators** start to cut away the coal. Dragline excavators are like cranes with a vast bucket at the front, which is lowered to the surface and then pulled toward the excavator with a dragline so it gouges up the coal. The excavator swings around and dumps the coal onto a conveyor or waiting truck, then turns back to take another bite. Bucket wheel excavators have a huge rotating wheel with many buckets, on the end of a long arm. The arm swings against the vertical coal "cliff" or face and eats its way in, with the coal falling onto a conveyor. The whole excavator moves along on tank-like caterpillar tracks or huge "feet."

### Big Muskie

Dragline excavators for coal mines are among the biggest moveable machines ever built. Ohio's "Big Muskie" was almost 400 feet (120 meters) long, 222 feet (68 meters) high, and weighed over 13,000 tons (11,800 metric tons). Its bucket held more than 300 tons (270 metric tons) of coal. It was in action from 1969 to 1991, when it was retired because the mines it worked produced coal unsuited to new environmental laws. In 1999, "Big Muskie" was cut up, providing enough steel to make the equivalent of 9,000 cars.

**A dragline excavator at a coal mine.**

In strip mining, or area mining, which is best for shallow, level coal seams, the process takes place in a series of strips—long, trench-like holes, one next to another.

As coal is cut from one strip, the overburden is cleared ahead of it, and then put into the dug-out area behind it, known as backfill. About two-thirds of US surface mines use this method.

Open pit mining uses similar machines to dig coal from a huge hole or pit, which gets wider and deeper until the coal runs out. Contour mining follows the coal seam along the contour or slope of a hillside. Again overburden is removed, the coal excavated, and the overburden and leftovers, or spoil, from the second cut fills the first one. This style is typical of rolling hills with exposed coal seams, as in the Appalachian Mountains. Less common methods are pit mines, augers, and dredging (see sidebar).

Another more recent method is mountaintop removal (MTR), or mountaintop mining (MTM). If there are coal seams in

**Rarer Forms of Surface Mining**

- **Pit mines** have narrow holes or pits dug into steeply dipping coal seams.
- **Auger mining** uses an auger—a huge drill-type device like a massive corkscrew, perhaps 7 feet (2 meters) wide. It churns into the seam and carries the coal out.
- In **dredging**, coal or other minerals are scooped up by a crane with a large bucket, which sits on a floating ship or barge.

the lower levels of a hill or mountain, the soil and rocks above—perhaps 1,000 feet (almost 300 meters) high—are "sliced off" by diggers and excavators, as overburden. The exposed coal is then dug out. In some areas, the overburden is dumped into nearby valleys or hollows. The result is that the whole landscape is flattened. The overburden may also be replaced in an effort to remake a hill or mountain, lower than the original, as an attempt at "rehabilitation." This mining method has caused huge controversy, as explained later.

## Underground (Deep) Mining

Several types of mine are used to get at coal seems deep underground. In a *drift mine,* the tunnel goes straight into a hillside. In a *slope mine,* the tunnel angles down to follow a sloping coal seam. In a *shaft mine,* vertical tunnels or "shafts" go straight down. Usually there are two or more shafts, for workers and machines to go in, for coal to come out, and for ventilation so that fresh air is brought in and any dangerous gases, like methane, are removed. Many shaft mines are less than 1,000 feet (300 meters) underground, but some go much deeper.

In *longwall* or *panel* mining, a machine moves along a wall-like coal face, digging or gouging or scraping off the coal. Usually this falls onto a conveyor that runs alongside the face and takes it to one end for removal. For safety, the rock surface above the face is held up by table-like metal plates on hydraulic rams that press on the roof. These roof supports are put up in stages, with the whole system advancing as the block-like panel is cut back. Left behind is the unsupported roof over a chamber-like empty area called the goaf, where coal once was. Here the roof is usually allowed to collapse in a safe, controlled way. The whole process hardly pauses and is known as continuous mining.

**An open-pit coal mine in the Rocky Mountains.**

Longwall panels can be over 1,000 feet (300 meters) wide and carry on into the seam for 10 times that distance. Modern longwall machines remove over 5,000 tons (4,535 metric tons) of coal per hour. The coal travels along the conveyor or in wagons, perhaps to a crushing machine, depending on lump size. It then continues up to the surface, either on a sloping conveyor, in railed wagons, or up a coal elevator. Longwall mining accounts for up to one-third of total US coal production.

## Room-and-Pillar Mining

A different underground method is called *room and pillar mining*. Here, coal is cut away to form rooms—also called stalls—leaving wide, block-like pillars or columns to support the roof and rocks above. The coal-cutting machines work in a similar way to those used in longwall mining. The sizes of the rooms and pillars, and their spacing, are carefully calculated to make sure the roof stays up. Rooms are typically 20–30 feet (6–9 meters) wide and pillars as wide as 100 feet (30 meters). As mining advances, a grid-like pattern of rooms and pillars forms. Sometimes more than half of the coal can be removed, with the rest of the area left as pillars.

In some cases, when the mining reaches the limits of a coal seam, the equipment may cut more coal on the way back. This is known as retreat mining, but it makes the pillars smaller, so it must be done very carefully since it increases risks of roof collapse.

Modern coal mines teem with sensors, control panels, computers, and safety equipment to guard against dangers such as roof collapse, or build-up of dangerous gases. Much of the process is automatic, allowing the miners stay away from the most hazardous areas.

### Deep Coal Mines

The Tower Mine, while it was in operation, was one of the deepest coal mines in the United States. Sited near Price, Utah, the Tower Mine went down 2,750 feet (838 meters). It was closed in 2008 due to safety concerns. The Springhill Mine in Nova Scotia, Canada, went down to a depth of some 4,400 feet (1,340 meters). It closed in 1958.

Coal mines in other parts of the world go even deeper. The Jindřich II Mine in the Czech Republic had a shaft more than 4,700 feet (1,430 meters) deep.

An illuminated tunnel in an underground coal mine.

## TEXT-DEPENDENT QUESTIONS

1. What is overburden, and how is it removed?
2. How long are longwall coal faces?
3. What is retreat mining?

## RESEARCH PROJECTS

1. Find out more about machines that cut coal in longwall mines. How fast do they travel, and how often do they stop for service and maintenance?
2. Look up information on the biggest coal mines that have produced the most coal over the years. Are they in North America?

## Chapter Three

# USING COAL

**Words to Understand**

**emissions:** substances given off by burning or similar chemical changes.

**flue gases:** gases produced by burning and other processes that come out of flues, stacks, chimneys, and similar outlets.

**ore:** a rock or similar natural material that contains large amounts of a valuable metal or mineral, such as iron or sulfur.

**oxides:** chemicals that contain oxygen combined with other substances.

**producer gas:** a gas created ("produced") by industrial rather than natural means.

**scrubber:** a device for removing, or "scrubbing," unwanted substances.

When coal finally sees the light of day, what happens next depends on its quality and grade, and on how it will be transported and used. In both surface and underground mining, the coal may go straight to a process called coal preparation at the mine site. The coal preparation plant, or prep plant, receives "raw" coal direct from the mine, called run-of-mine (ROM) coal. It is basically crushed into convenient-sized lumps and cleaned or "washed" into a purer form. Siting the prep plant at the mine makes it more cost-effective to transport.

In addition to the leftovers from coal mining itself, called spoil or gob, coal preparation produces great quantities of wastes, with names such as tailings, middlings, and slurry. These have to be safely recycled or disposed, adding to coal's cost and environmental problems.

**Coal being transported by train.**

Finally the prepared coal is taken, usually by conveyor, to bins, silos, or hill-sized stockpiles. It may also be loaded straight into trucks, trains, barges, or bulk carrier cargo ships. Coal, being fairly heavy solid lumps, is costly to transport, especially so compared to petroleum oil and natural gas, which flow along pipelines.

## Power Generation

More than nine-tenths of coal use in North America is to generate electricity in power plants. The coal burns in enormous furnaces. It heats water in a boiler into steam at

**About 90 percent of America's coal is used to power electrical plants.**

very high pressure. The steam blasts past the angled, fan-like blades of a turbine and makes them spin around on their shaft (axle), which also carries the wire coils of the generator. As the coils spin around in a powerful magnetic field, electricity flows through the wires and is led away for use.

Coal-fired power plants are massive structures that operate at very high temperatures and pressures. The coal is stored in great piles and must be supplied continuously to the furnace. But it is not burned as lumps. It is pulverized or ground up into tiny particles or powders, which are dried by heat from the furnace. The pulverized powder is then blown through nozzles to mix with fan-blown, preheated air in the furnace chamber. Here the coal particles burn very hot and fast in a "fireball" in the middle of the furnace, at temperatures up to 1,300°F (700°C).

The boiler part is not so much a single container for water, like a kettle on a hotplate. It is, rather, a network of thousands of feet of pipes known as a "water wall" forming the sides of the furnace, each pipe around 2–3 inches (5–8 centimeters) wide. These pick up heat from the burning coal and turn the water inside them into steam. There are various sets of pipes, such as superheaters and reheaters, that make the whole process more effective. This gets the most heat energy from the coal and increases the steam pressure so it spins the turbine blades more powerfully. The whole furnace-boiler structure can be more than 60 feet (18 meters) wide and 150 feet (46 meters) tall.

> ## Coal on the High Seas
>
> The ships called bulk carriers are, like oil tankers, some of the biggest vessels afloat. The largest are over 1,000 feet (300 meters) long and 200 feet (60 meters) wide, and hold more than 400,000 tons (360,000 metric tons) of cargo. Along with coal, they can carry various "dry" loads, such as ore rocks, cements, and grains.

## Power Plant Emissions

Burning coal in power plant furnaces produces gas **emissions** that come out of the furnace flue, stack, or chimney, which may be 500 feet (150 meters) high. These **flue gases** are mainly carbon dioxide, sulfur dioxide, and nitrogen **oxides**. Carbon dioxide

**An emissions scrubber at a coal-fired plant in North Carolina.**

($CO_2$) is formed by the combination of carbon from the coal and oxygen from the air. The other oxides form in a similar way. There are also ash particles that are very small and fly out with the gas emissions, as well as heavier particles that fall into a collection area. Fly ash can be caught by devices called electrostatic precipitators. They use static electricity to make the tiny particles clump into larger, heavier ones, which then fall and can be collected. Another method is to pass the emissions through a filter that traps the particles.

The gaseous emissions from burning coal, and other fossil fuels—in fact, from any fuel that burns—are a significant problem. To cut down on these troubles, power generators in North America must have filters and **scrubbers** to remove the pollutants from the air. In a wet scrubber, fine droplets of a chemical are sprayed into the flue gases. This may be calcium carbonate (as in limestone), calcium hydroxide (as in lime) or a similar chemical. The droplets react with the gases to make solids that can be collected. In the spray-dry method, by contrast, jets of heated air turn the polluting chemicals into a dry, powdery substance.

## Metallurgic Coal

The other main usage of coal is for making iron and steel. When coal is used in this way, it's referred to as *metallurgic* or *coking* coal—that is, coal converted into coke. Coke is a hard black or grey substance created by heating bituminous coking coal to extremely high temperatures in an anaerobic environment. Because there is no oxygen, the coal can't burn. Instead of burning, it is transformed by heat, in a process called destructive distillation, into an array of substances, including coal tar, ammonia liquor, and coal gas. At the end of the process, all that remains is coke. All of these products are useful in industry.

Coke contains more carbon (up to 95 percent) than the original bituminous coal. It burns more effectively and hotter, with a heat content similar to anthracite, at 12,000–13,500 BTUs per pound. Also, in terms of its chemistry, it acts as a reducing agent—a substance that removes oxygen. So it is both a primary fuel and reducing agent for smelting, which means

> ### Leftovers
>
> Treating of 1 ton (0.9 metric tons) of coal by destructive distillation can produce:
> - 1,700 pounds (770 kilograms) of coke
> - 30 US gallons (115 liters) of coal tar
> - 15 US gallons (57 liters) of ammonia liquor
> - 14,000 cubic feet (400 cubic meters) of coal gas

obtaining metals from ore rocks using heat and chemical reduction. In a blast furnace, coke is mixed with iron **ore**, such as hematite, and limestone, and heated to temperatures of 3,000°F (1,650°C). The coke burns in air to make carbon monoxide gas, and this takes away the oxygen from hematite to leave a form of iron called pig iron, which is the basis of steelmaking and other iron industries. Coke is also a fuel in smelting plants for copper, silver, and other metals.

The anthracite industry in North America is far smaller than the bituminous coal industry, and almost all the anthracite comes from Pennsylvania. Its main uses are in smelting metal ores; as an efficient, almost smokeless fuel for heating; in the electrical industry; and for water filters.

**Close view of a blast furnace used in making iron.**

## Other Uses of Coal

Gases that burn as fuels are obtained from coal in very different ways. One is a natural release of gas from coal seams—especially methane, which is the main substance that also occurs in natural gas. It is called *coal bed methane* or *coal seam methane*. Another gas is carbon dioxide. These and other gases are together known as coal seam gases (CSGs). They formed in the coal as part of coalification, existing under great pressure in water and other liquids. When coal is mined or drilled into, the pressure releases and the gases bubble out   like taking the top off a soda bottle.

Coal bed methane can be extracted by drilling down through rocks to the coal seams below, in a similar way to drilling for petroleum oil or natural gas. The main states for coal bed methane are Colorado, Wyoming, and New Mexico. This methane is a fairly small proportion, less than 1/20th, of the natural gas produced in North America. There is a problem with the process, however. As the gas comes out of the well, so do great amounts of water, known as "produced water," and this water often carries toxic substances. Cleaning and disposing of it is a costly business.

Burnable gas fuels are also derived from yield coal gas, or town gas, which is one type of **producer gas**. Coal gas contains around 10 percent carbon monoxide, 30 percent methane, and 50 percent hydrogen. These all burn, and coal gas was formerly a widespread fuel for cooking, heating, and light before the development of natural gas production in North America during the 1940s and 1950s.

The general process for obtaining gases from coal is known as coal gasification, though there are several other methods. Some involve heating coal while air or oxygen, and perhaps steam (water vapor), pass through—but not enough for proper burning or combustion. This can be done in a plant known as a coal refinery, working along similar principles to an oil refinery. Or it may be carried out by drilling down

### "Ready-Made" Coal

Coal from the largest-producing US state, Wyoming, naturally has a low sulfur and ash content. This makes it simpler to prepare, sometimes by crushing alone, and burning it produces less sulfur oxides, too. So it is highly suited as thermal coal for electricity generation. Over 95 percent of Wyoming coal is used to produce electricity in more than 20 US states.

## Other Coal Products

Coal is also used in the making of many other products, including:

- various products made by paper, chemical, and pharmaceutical industries
- creosote oil, naphthalene, phenol, and benzene
- ammonia products such as nitric acid and agricultural fertilizers
- solvents, dyes, fibers, and plastics
- activated carbon in water and air filters
- carbon fiber in mountain bikes, tennis racquets, racing cars, and similar products
- cement, concrete, and other construction materials
- cosmetics, hair shampoos, and toothpastes
- lubricants, water repellents, and resins

into coal seams, pumping in oxygen or air under pressure, and collecting the coal gas. This can be burned as fuel or, in many cases, changed into yet another form, called syngas, or synthesis gas. Syngas is mainly hydrogen and carbon monoxide, and it has various uses as a fuel in power plants, factories, and vehicles.

The coal gasification process is evolving all the time. Coal gas can be routed to making intermediate substances for gasoline and diesel production, or to produce hydrogen for the chemical industry and hydrogen-fuelled vehicles. Yet another outcome can be methane-based synthetic natural gas (SNG), also called substitute natural gas, which is used in the same way as regular natural gas. And there is another group of processes called direct coal-to-liquids (CTL), where coal is converted by various chemical means to liquid fuels such as gasoline and diesel, without the between stage of gasifying.

Many of the coal-based technologies discussed above are interlinked, with the product from one becoming the raw material for the next. This is part of the shift to use the plentiful natural resource of coal in cleaner, more efficient ways. However, at present, nine-tenths of North American coal still is burned to generate electricity.

## TEXT-DEPENDENT QUESTIONS

1. What are the different uses of steaming coal and coking coal?
2. What is produced water?
3. What are the differences between coal gas and syngas?

## RESEARCH PROJECTS

1. Look up information on coal transport. What kinds of special care does this cargo need, for example, in terms of fire risk?
2. Find out more about syngas. Why is it known as "synthesis gas," and how does it differ from SNG, synthetic natural gas?

## Chapter Four

# THE COAL INDUSTRY

## Words to Understand

**automation:** making a process automatic, done by machines that largely control themselves, rather than being controlled by people.

**fracking:** hydraulic fracturing, a process of breaking up a substance using high-pressure fluids.

North America's coal industry produces about 1,000 million tons (900 million metric tons) annually. It is bested in size only by China—although China produces three times this amount. Coal is present in about 38 US states and covers an area up to one-eighth of the whole country. Bituminous coal is mainly in the Appalachian regions of the East and the Midwest, while coals from the West and South are mostly sub-bituminous. Canada is about the 15th largest coal producer in the world, at 65–70 million tons (58–63 million metric tons) each year. Its reserves are largely in Alberta and are the world's 12th largest. Mexico, too, has a coal industry, but it is comparatively small, producing 16–17 million tons (14–15 million metric tons) annually.

Since the start of the Industrial Revolution and the discovery of North American coal reserves, in the late 18th and early 19th centuries, coal has been a huge part of the energy business and a way of life for millions of people. Over this period, its uses spread to iron and steel making, railroad locomotives, factory furnaces, ovens and kilns, home heating, and countless other consumer uses. In 1882, coal powered North America's first plant to generate electricity for public users—Thomas Edison's Pearl Street Station in New York. That was the beginning of coal's massive use by the electricity industry.

## A Century of Coal

By 1920, total US coal production had reached almost 700 million tons (630 million metric tons), about two-thirds of today's level. At that time, the United States had

**Coal miners taking a lunch break more than 2 miles below ground, in 1910.**

around 650,000 workers in the coal industry, compared to some 90,000 in the early 21st century. (For a comparison, that is about the same as the number in the wind power industry, while the solar energy industry employs over 140,000 workers.) Mining, transporting, and burning coal were tough, dirty jobs. Accidents in deep mines were all too common, and many lost their lives, while others developed lung, skin, and other diseases from exposure to coal dust and similar substances.

The coal industry was one of the first where workers grouped together to form labor unions, so that they could campaign for better pay and working conditions.

**The remains of the strikers' camp in Ludlow, Colorado, after it was burned down by National Guardsmen in 1914.**

Along with from other industries, such as cotton and textiles, construction, and railroads, they organized labor stoppages or strikes. In 1897, in Lattimer, Pennsylvania, 19 miners were killed and at least 39 were wounded during a union march. In May 1902, anthracite miners in Pennsylvania began a strike. As it dragged on, the economic effects were so severe that in October, President Theodore Roosevelt summoned the employers and workers to Washington, DC. This strike was the first time the US government became directly involved in helping to settle a labor dispute.

Problems continued, however, with more mining strikes and deaths. In 1914, in Ludlow, Colorado, the National Guard and Colorado Fuel and Iron Company guards killed more than 20 men, women, and children when they set fire to a tented village of striking miner families. In Sydney, Nova Scotia, in 1923, miners went on strike in support of steelworkers. The disputes continued for three years, with much violence, and thousands of Canadian troops were sent to control the situation. In 1925, a miner named William Davis was shot dead, leading to the William Davis Miners' Memorial Day on June 11 each year. Coal industry strikes continued into the 1970s and 1980s, though they were much reduced in number. Because of this troubled history, coal

## US Coal Production, 2013

| State | Million Tons (Metric Tons) of Coal | Percent of Total US Production |
|---|---|---|
| Wyoming | 388 (350) | 40 |
| West Virginia | 113 (102) | 11 |
| Kentucky | 79 (71) | 8 |
| Pennsylvania | 54 (49) | 6 |
| Illinois | 52 (47) | 5 |
| Texas | 42 (38) | 4 |
| Montana | 42 (38) | 4 |
| Indiana | 39 (36) | 4 |
| North Dakota | 28 (25) | 3 |
| Ohio | 25 (23) | 3 |

A giant excavator tears away at the ground at an open-pit lignite (brown coal) mine.

mining has a special place in the social history of North America, as it does in Europe, Russia, and other regions.

## Modern Trends

Coal provides almost two-fifths of all energy used in the United States, with over 500 coal-fuelled power plants in operation. The coal industry continues to be both a major employer and provider of energy and raw materials. The industry is making efforts to lessen coal's problems by using better pollution control methods, as well as the combined or integrated technologies described in the next chapter.

### Importing Coal?

The United States seems to have so much coal—so why bring it in from elsewhere? But for big coal users on the Gulf Coast and along the southern Atlantic Coast, it can cost less to ship coal from places such as Colombia, where it is also cheaper to produce, than to transport it from mining areas in the United States.

However, the number of workers in the mining and coal industries has fallen, mainly due to **automation**. Mining is also less widespread, with only four states—Wyoming, West Virginia, Kentucky, and Pennsylvania—providing two-thirds of all US coal. In recent years, the total amount of coal mined has fallen slightly. Meanwhile, the amount of electricity generated by coal has been reduced from almost one-half of the total to about one-third.

There are a number of reasons for these trends. One is the awareness that burning any fuels, and especially fossil fuels, is a major cause of pollution and climate change. Coal produces higher amounts of polluting substances than other fuels, such as natural gas. In addition, new environmental laws make it more costly to build and operate coal plants. In 2011, President Barack Obama urged the country to develop more clean energy sources with little or no carbon dioxide pollution; Canada has been following this path for many years. Also, natural gas has recently become much more available due to technologies such as **fracking**. And the share of energy provided by renewables such as solar, wind, and water is rising.

However, the proportion of US coal exported to other regions, mainly Europe and Asia, is rising slowly. The United Kingdom takes the largest share of steam coal, while Brazil imports the most coking coal. Anti-coal campaigners argue that the

## Top 10 Coal-Producing Nations

The top nations for coal production, with annual production amounts, are as follows (annual amounts are averaged over recent years):

- China: 3,000 million tons (2,700 million metric tons)
- United States: 1,000 million tons (900 million metric tons)
- India: 600 million tons (540 million metric tons)
- Australia: 410 million tons (370 million metric tons)
- Russia: 310 million tons (280 million metric tons)
- Indonesia: 270 million tons (245 million metric tons)
- South Africa: 270 million tons (245 million metric tons)
- Poland: 150 million tons (135 million metric tons)
- Kazakhstan: 110 million tons (99 million metric tons)
- Colombia: 85 million tons (77 million metric tons)

United States is exporting pollution by sending this "dirty fuel" to other nations where environmental laws are less strict. Supporters of coal, meanwhile, argue that it is a vast and valuable North American natural resource and that the coal industry should be allowed to evolve new methods and technologies.

## TEXT-DEPENDENT QUESTIONS

1. When and where was coal first used to generate electricity for public use?
2. What was President Roosevelt's role in the Anthracite Coal Strike of 1902?
3. Why is the proportion of electricity produced from coal falling?

## RESEARCH PROJECTS

1. What are the links between coal mining and Labor Day in the United States and Labour Day in Canada?
2. Are the trends seen in the North American coal industry happening elsewhere in the world, such as Europe, China, India, and South America?

## Chapter Five

# COAL AND THE ENVIRONMENT

### Words to Understand

**sequestration:** storing or taking something to keep it for a time.

**spoil heaps:** piles of material left over from excavation.

**subsidence:** sinking lower or falling, as when land sinks above an old coal mine.

**watercourse:** a channel along which water flows, such as a brook, creek, or river.

For some people, coal is a major villain in today's industrial world. They see it as a huge cause of pollution for land, air, and water, and as a great producer of greenhouse gases—which it is, worldwide. To counter these problems, the coal industry in North America is working to lessen pollution and to increase the use of coal as a valuable raw material, as well as a fuel that ensures the continent of energy supplies well into the future.

## Greenhouse Gas

Almost any kind of burning produces carbon dioxide. It is called a greenhouse gas because, in the atmosphere, it helps to trap and hold heat—much like the panes of glass in a greenhouse. Along with other greenhouse gases, such as methane, carbon dioxide is causing the surface temperature of the Earth to rise, a phenomenon termed *global warming*. Nearly all scientists now agree that global warming is here, that it is increasing, that it is caused by human activities—chiefly, burning fossil fuels.

In North America, carbon dioxide accounts for about four-fifths of all greenhouse gas emissions. About one-third of this carbon dioxide comes from electricity generation, and coal creates around two-fifths of these emissions. Taking into account other coal uses, coal is responsible for broadly 30 to 35 percent of US greenhouse gas emissions. (Similar calculations show that petroleum oil is the source of up to 40 percent of US greenhouse gas emissions.)

Methane constitutes around one-tenth of North America's greenhouse gas emissions. Methane is very powerful—it is more than 20 times more effective at trapping heat than carbon dioxide over a time span of 100 years. However, methane does not last in the atmosphere as long as carbon dioxide does. So its greenhouse effects are bigger over a short period, while carbon dioxide's are not as big but last longer, since it persists for 100 to 200 years. Low-level methane seeping from surface

### A Warmer Earth

Global warming is predicted not only to make the Earth's air, land, and water hotter, but also to change patterns of weather, create more storms and other extreme events, bring droughts and floods to new regions, and warm the oceans, which will kill corals and marine life. It will melt glaciers and ice caps to raise the sea level and flood vast low-lying areas. And there are probably many more, as yet unknown, effects of global warming.

and underground coal mines is part of the methane emission problem. Overall, coal mining accounts for 10 percent of North America's human-related methane emissions. By comparison, methane from decay in waste landfills is nearer 20 percent, the digestive gas from farm livestock is responsible for 25 percent; and the natural gas and petroleum industries are responsible for closer to 30 percent.

## Carbon Reduction

Industries that burn fuels such as coal, petroleum oil, and natural gas are developing carbon capture and storage (CCS) technology—also known as carbon capture and **sequestration**. This is a major new technology that traps carbon dioxide using several methods. For coal-fired power plants, carbon is collected from flue gases in a process similar to scrubbing, described previously, where the gas dissolves in a liquid. The liquid would be treated for controlled release of the carbon dioxide and recycled to collect more. The released carbon dioxide gas could then be sent along pipelines or in bulk gas carrier ships, as natural gas, to where it is stored—somewhere hopefully out of harm's way and for a very long time. Such places include deep rock formations or old, used-up petroleum oil and natural gas areas.

The whole field of CCS is just beginning. The United States has created seven Regional Carbon Sequestration Partnerships (RCSPs) across the nation to help develop the technology. Canada also has several large-scale trials. The Weyburn Project takes carbon dioxide through a pipeline from a coal gasification plant in Beulah, North Dakota, some 200 miles (320 kilometers) away, and injects in into the Weyburn-Midale oilfield, in Saskatchewan, to make more oil come to the surface.

Another approach is to make the sequence of burning coal to generate electricity more efficient and less polluting. In an integrated gasification combined cycle (IGCC) plant, coal is first dried and gasified to make syngas. Syngas may be purified and burned in a "cleaner" way for electricity generation. At every stage, pollution is minimized, and energy and materials are recycled as much as possible. The Edwardsport Power Station in Knox County, Indiana, is one of the first IGCCs to use large-scale IGCC in the United States. It started up in 2013 and may eventually power as many as half a million homes. However, its design and building have been controversial—there have been management problems, increasing costs, and planning conflicts between project leaders and state officials.

## "Dirty" Coal

Coal releases many other unwanted substances when burned. The sulfur and nitrogen oxides and hydrogen chloride cause problems because they are acidic gases. As they spread into the atmosphere, they dissolve in water droplets in clouds, and then in rain

**The environmental impacts of coal are not limited to North America. This photo of Shanghai, China, shows the smog problem that plagues some parts of that country. In the foreground, coal barges carry more of the resources to power plants.**

**Liquid waste at an open-pit coal mine.**

to make it acidic, too. This "acid rain" damages trees and other plants, and it collects in streams, rivers, and lakes, harming fish and other wildlife. The heavy metals cause long-standing, well-known problems in the environment, harming both wildlife and human health.

Coal is not alone in causing these issues. But coal's wide use in the United States, and its even wider use in other parts of the world, make it a major contributor. To address the problems, North American coal-burning facilities are among world leaders in scrubbing, filtering, and generally controlling such emissions. However, many clean-air campaigners want faster progress, or say that coal has had its day and cannot keep up with the latest laws on atmosphere pollution.

## Coal Mining and the Environment

Even before coal is burned, mining it brings many environmental challenges. Few people want a giant surface coal mine near their home. There can be worries such as soil erosion, dust, noise, traffic, water pollution, **subsidence**, hugely altered landscapes, and effects on local wildlife. Modern North American mines work hard to minimize these impacts, with a view to rehabilitation, or putting the area back to its original state, as far as possible. But on an even larger scale, mountaintop mining has altered whole landscapes, removed their wildlife, polluted water, and generally caused environmental changes on a vast scale. Many campaign groups are challenging this process, while the coal corporations say it will be an advantage in the long term.

In surface mining, the soil can be stored in embankments around the mine site to reduce unsightly views, noise, and dust. Vehicles have silencers, and water sprays also reduce dust. There may also be an opportunity to include a landfill for municipal solid waste, which always has to go somewhere. At the end of the mine's life, the operators are usually bound by law to restore the area to farmland, forestry, recreation, or wilderness.

Underground mining operations also have environmental impacts. There are **spoil heaps**, the risk of methane buildup, water pollution, and subsidence. Spoil heaps are planned to be landscaped by planting trees and returning the original scenery, as

This photo, taken in Logan, West Virginia, in 1974, shows a massive spoil heap burning just a short distance from the miners' homes. Modern companies try to do a better job handling the leftovers of coal mining, but spoil remains an issue.

is also the case for surface mining. Preventing subsidence, or sinking, is far from an exact science, but again modern geology studies can make it far less likely.

Water pollution from coal mines is also a difficult issue. Most underground mines, and even some surface sites, are below the water table. As the water in the rocks, called groundwater, slowly moves through them, the action of chemical changes and bacterial microbes may make it acidic. This may only be detected years later, when the mine is closed. The polluted water can eventually reach the surface, nearby or even far away, and damage **watercourses**, wildlife, and habitats. This acid mine drainage (AMD) is much reduced with modern methods, but it has left lasting scars in many older mining regions. A similar problem comes from old surface piles of coal waste tips, spoil, tailings, and similar leftovers.

## Safety Concerns

The bad old days of frequent, large-scale mining disasters are largely in the past, at least in North America. The greatest dangers were from collapse and the dreaded firedamp, or methane. Undetected by human eyes, ears, or noses, this gas can seep out of the walls and collect in pockets. If it reaches a proportion of 5 to 15 percent in the air, the slightest spark from any electrical equipment can set off raging fires or outright explosions.

North American coal mining has worked to reduce this and other risks. Geology experts and mechanical, electronic, and chemical sensors monitor the tunnels and coal faces for any slight shift in the surrounding rocks, "sniffing" for methane and other gases, and constantly checking for air problems. Ventilation equipment, too, is improving all the time. But, as with any heavy industry, from oil rig flare-ups to chemical factory leaks, coal mining still suffers accidents.

## The Future of Coal

Around the world, the pattern of energy sources and uses is changing fast. Many nations are pushing toward more renewable energy, reduced greenhouse gases and other toxic emissions, and less damage to the environment, wildlife, and human health. Renewables also give energy security in that each nation provides for its own needs, rather than buying energy from other countries, which can be affected by global prices, trade bans, and even wars.

Coal's supporters argue that this natural resource already gives North America energy independence. It is plentiful and relatively cheap. Further, technologies are being developed to make it less polluting as a burned fuel, so that modern mining

### Mining Disasters

Few events grab the news more than coal mine fires, explosions, collapses, and other accidents. These are a few significant ones:

- Canada's worst single disaster was at the Hillcrest Mine, Alberta, in 1914, when 189 workers died in an explosion.
- In 1992, 26 miners died in a methane explosion at the Westray Mine in Plymouth, Nova Scotia—which had only opened the previous year.
- The deadliest event in the United States was at Monongah Mine, West Virginia, in 1907. At least 360 miners were killed in a fireball due to burning coal dust or methane. In 2010, 29 miners lost their lives at the Upper Big Branch Mine in Montcoal, West Virginia. Again, a probable mix of coal dust and methane caught fire and set off a series of explosions.

**Families in Tallsmanville, West Virginia comfort each other in 2006, after an explosion trapped 13 miners underground.  Only one miner survived.**

is far less harmful to the environment than it once was. Coal is not only an energy resource, it can also provide many kinds of raw materials and products. It powered the Industrial Revolution and has been central to industries and products that are now widespread and important for modern life.

In the past few years, the United States and Canada have passed new, stricter regulations to reduce greenhouse and toxic gas emissions, not only from new fossil-fuelled power plants but also from existing ones. Natural gas, which burns relatively clean and is becoming much more available, can perhaps be a "bridge" energy source to the real long-term future of renewables. Coal has a long, vital, and famous past. Its role in the coming decades and centuries is less clear.

## TEXT-DEPENDENT QUESTIONS

1. Which fossil fuel is responsible for more US greenhouse gas emissions— coal, natural gas, or petroleum oil?
2. What does IGCC mean?
3. What is firedamp?

## RESEARCH PROJECTS

1. Look up worldwide information on which nations are leading the move from fossil fuels to renewables. How are the United States, Canada, and Mexico involved?
2. Research the notion of energy independence. How does North America today compare to, say, 50 years ago, and what's expected in 50 years' time?

"To waste, to destroy, our natural resources, to skin and exhaust the land instead of using it so as to increase its usefulness, will result in undermining in the days of our children the very prosperity which we ought by right to hand down to them amplified and developed."

—Theodore Roosevelt
President of the United States (1901 to 1909)
Seventh Annual Message
December 3, 1907

# Further Reading

## BOOKS

Doeden, Matt. *Finding Out about Coal, Oil, and Natural Gas.* Searchlight Books:
    What Are Energy Sources? Minneapolis, MN: Lerner Publications, 2014.

Freese, Barbara. *Coal: A Human History.* Cambridge, MA: Perseus Books, 2003.

Gogerly, Liz. *Fossil Fuels.* A World After. Chicago: Heinemann, 2014.

Horn, Geoffrey M., and Debra Voege. *Coal, Oil, and Natural Gas.* Energy Today. New
    York: Chelsea House, 2010.

Marcovitz, Hal. *What Is the Future of Fossil Fuels?* Future of Renewable Energy. San
    Diego, CA: ReferencePoint Press, 2013.

Pipe, Jim. *Coal: The Big Polluter?* World Energy Issues. London: Franklin Watts, 2010.

Simon, Seymour. *Global Warming.* New York: HarperCollins, 2013.

## ONLINE

American Coal Foundation. "Coal Energy Facts."
    http://teachcoal.org/coal-energy-facts.

Energy Kids. "Coal Basics." US Energy Information Administration.
    http://www.eia.gov/kids/energy.cfm?page=coal_home-basics.

National Geographic. "Coal." http://education.nationalgeographic.co.uk/education/
    encyclopedia/coal.

# Series Glossary

**alloy:** mixture of two or more metals.

**alluvial:** relating to soil that is deposited by running water.

**aquicludes:** layers of rocks through which groundwater cannot flow.

**aquifer:** an underground water source.

**archeologists:** scientists who study ancient cultures by examining their material remains, such as buildings, tools, and other artifacts.

**biodegradable:** the process by which bacteria and organisms naturally break down a substance.

**biodiversity:** the variety of life; all the living things in an area, or on Earth on the whole.

**by-product:** a substance or material that is not the main desired product of a process but happens to be made along the way.

**carbon:** a pure chemical substance or element, symbol C, found in great amounts in living and once-living things.

**catalyst:** a substance that speeds up a chemical change or reaction that would otherwise happen slowly, if at all.

**commodity:** an item that is bought and sold.

**compound:** two or more elements chemically bound together.

**constituent:** ingredient; one of the parts of a whole.

**contaminated:** polluted with harmful substances.

**convection:** circular motion of a liquid or gas resulting from temperature differences.

**corrosion:** the slow destruction of metal by various chemical processes.

**dredge:** a machine that can remove material from under water.

**emissions:** substances given off by burning or similar chemical changes.

**excavator:** a machine, usually with one or more toothed wheels or buckets that digs material out of the ground.

**flue gases:** gases produced by burning and other processes that come out of flues, stacks, chimneys, and similar outlets.

**forges:** makes or shapes metal by heating it in furnaces or beating or hammering it.

**fossil fuels:** sources of fuel, such as oil and coal, that contain carbon and come from the decomposed remains of prehistoric plants and animals.

**fracking:** shorthand for hydraulic fracturing, a method of extracting gas and oil from rocks.

**fusion:** energy generated by joining two or more atoms.

**geologists:** scientists who study Earth's structure or that of another planet.

**greenhouse gas:** a gas that helps to trap and hold heat—much like the panes of glass in a greenhouse.

**hydrocarbon:** a substance containing only the pure chemical substances, or elements, carbon and hydrogen.

**hydrologic cycle:** events in which water vapor condenses and falls to the surface as rain, snow, or sleet, and then evaporates and returns to the atmosphere.

**indigenous:** growing or living naturally in a particular region or environment.

**inorganic:** compound of minerals rather than living material.

**kerogens:** a variety of substances formed when once-living things decayed and broke down, on the way to becoming natural gas or oil.

**leachate:** liquid containing wastes.

**mineralogists:** scientists who study minerals and how to classify, locate, and distinguish them.

**nonrenewable resources:** natural resources that are not replenished over time; these exist in fixed, limited supplies.

**ore:** naturally occurring mineral from which metal can be extracted.

**ozone:** a form of oxygen containing three atoms of oxygen in a molecule.

**porous:** allowing a liquid to seep or soak through small holes and channels.

**primordial:** existing at the beginning of time.

**producer gas:** a gas created ("produced") by industrial rather than natural means.

**reclamation:** returning something to its former state.

**reducing agent:** a substance that decreases another substance in a chemical reaction.

**refine:** to make something purer, or separate it into its various parts.

**remote sensing:** detecting and gathering information from a distance, for example, when satellites in space measure air and ground temperature below.

**renewable:** a substance that can be made, or a process used, again and again.

**reserves:** amounts in store, which can be used in the future.

**runoff:** water not absorbed by the soil that flows into lakes, streams, rivers, and oceans.

**seismology:** the study of waves, as vibrations or "shaking," that pass through the Earth's rocks, soils, and other structures.

**sequestration:** storing or taking something to keep it for a time.

**shaft:** a vertical passage that gives miners access to mine.

**sluice:** artificial water channel that is controlled by a value or gate.

**slurry:** a mixture of water and a solid that can't be dissolved.

**smelting:** the act of separating metal from rock by melting it at high temperatures

**subsidence:** the sinking down of land resulting from natural shifts or human activities.

**sustainable:** able to carry on for a very long time, at least the foreseeable future.

**synthesis:** making or producing something by adding substances together.

**tailing:** the waste product left over after ore has been extracted from rock.

**tectonic:** relating to the structure and movement of the earth's crust.

**watercourse:** a channel along which water flows, such as a brook, creek, or river.

# Index

(page numbers in *italics* refer to photographs and illustrations)

## About the Author

**Steve Parker** is an author and editor of children's non-fiction books and websites, chiefly in the areas of nature and the biological sciences. He has written more than 100 titles about the natural world, animals and plants, ecology, conservation, rocks and fossils, mineral wealth, and Earth's varied and valuable resources— and how human activities are affecting them, both historically and into the future. Steve's recent works include the *Animal Diaries* series (QED, London) about how our exploitation of land, water, air and the general environment affects the daily lives of creatures as diverse as a garden spider, lion, penguin, golden eagle and shark.

## Photo Credits

### Cover

Clockwise from left: iStock.com/jferrer; Dollar Photo Club/Oleksiy Mark; iStock.com/Philip_hens; Dollar Photo Club/bibi; Library of Congress; iStock.com/TjunctionMedia; iStock.com/TomasSereda.

### Interior

**Dollar Photo Club:** 11 Pedro Bigeriego; 22 John Casey; 36 Maxisport; 47 Alexander.
**Environmental Protection Agency:** 52.
**iStock.com:** 10 Maks08; 12 dbaer1970; 14 Adam88xx; 15 EmilyNorton; 19 indykb; 24 InStock; 26 Jacek_Sopotnicki; 29 kurmis; 30 IngaNielsen; 34 scanrail; 42 Miklav; 50 hsvrs; 54 EdStock.
**Library of Congress:** 39 Underwood & Underwood; 40 Bain News Service.
**Wikimedia Commons:** 20 Dvortygirl; 32 Murr Rhame; 49 Peter Dowley.